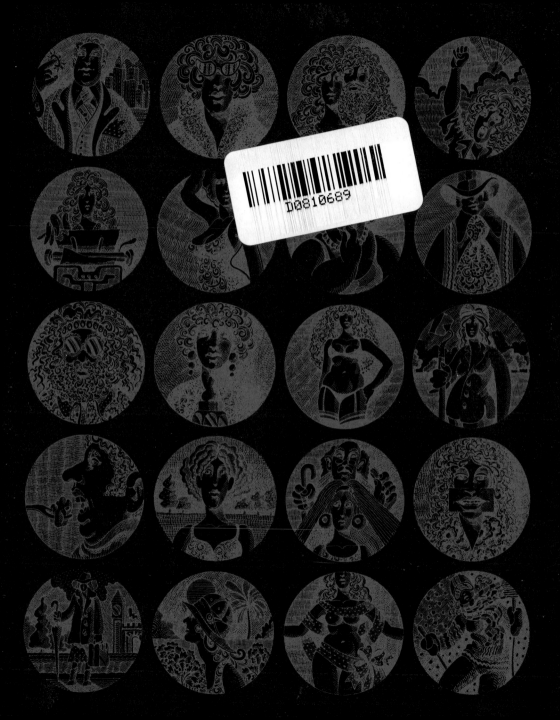

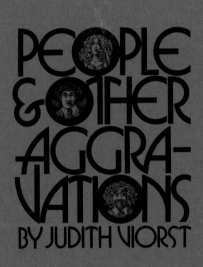

PEOPLE & OTHER AGGRAVATIONS

BY JUDITH VIORST

Illustrations by John Alcorn
Designed by Herb Lubalin & Annegret Beier

Books by Judith Viorst

PEOPLE & OTHER AGGRAVATIONS

BY JUDITH VIORST

The World Publishing Company
New York and Cleveland

Published by The World Publishing Company
Published simultaneously in Canada
by Nelson, Foster & Scott Ltd.
First printing 1971
Copyright © 1969, 1970, 1971 by Judith Viorst.
Library of Congress catalog card number: 70-145835
Printed in the United States of America
World Publishing
Times Mirror

This book is dedicated, with love, to Suzanne Aurelio,
Jean Boudin, Phyllis Hersh, Shay Rieger, and Elizabeth Rubenstein

CONTENTS

PEOPLE & OTHER AGGRAVATIONS

I'm having twelve for dinner and the butcher won't deliver.
I forgot my mother's birthday and she's brooding.
Computers keep on dunning me for bills I paid six months ago,
And I'm also including air pollution, Richard Nixon, germ
    warfare, the Pill, people...and other aggravations.

Penn Central only answers me with tape-recorded messages.
Our pre-school's split on cookies versus crackers.
The girl my husband hired is about to proposition him,
Not to mention hijackers, the S S T, race relations, the Joint
    Chiefs of Staff, people...and other aggravations.

My in-laws say my attitude is very uncooperative.
The dentist found my gums in poor condition.
The card I mailed a month ago still hasn't reached East Paterson,
And there are, in addition, the urban crisis, William Buckley, the
    sex revolution, inflation, people...and other aggravations.

The first-grade teacher tells me that my son said dirty things to her.
Don't ask what I would give to get a plumber.
The friends who just broke up insist I have to choose whose side I'm on,
Plus the long hot summer, overpopulation, John Birchers, the bomb,
    people...and other aggravations.

My forty-dollar Dynel braid is stuck with Double-Bubble gum.
The car (third time this week) has flunked inspection.
Our broker has advised me of some alternate insurance plans,
But none of them provides complete protection against
Cigarettes,
Cholesterol,
Weathermen,
The ABM,
CBS,
NBC,
Drug addiction,
DDT,
People...and other aggravations.

A WOMEN'S LIBERATION MOVEMENT WOMAN

When it's snowing and I put on all the galoshes
While he reads the paper,
Then I want to become a
Women's Liberation Movement woman.

14

And when it's snowing and he looks for the taxi
While I wait in the lobby,
Then I don't.
And when it's vacation and I'm in charge of mosquito bites
    and poison ivy and car sickness
While he's in charge of swimming,
Then I want to become a
Women's Liberation Movement woman.
And when it's vacation and he carries the trunk and the
    overnight bag and the extra blankets
While I carry the wig case,
Then I don't.
And when it's three in the morning and the baby definitely needs
    a glass of water and I have to get up and bring it
While he keeps my place warm,
Then I want to become a
Women's Liberation Movement woman.
And when it's three in the morning and there is definitely a
    murderer-rapist in the vestibule and he has to get up and catch him
While I keep his place warm,
Then I don't.

And after dinner, when he talks to the company
While I clean the broiler
(because I am a victim of capitalism, imperialism, male chauvinism,
    and also Playboy magazine),
And afternoons, when he invents the telephone and wins the Dreyfus
    case and writes War and Peace
While I sort the socks
(because I am economically oppressed, physically exploited,
    psychologically mutilated, and also very insulted),
And after he tells me that it is genetically determined that the
    man makes martinis and the lady makes the beds
(because he sees me as a sex object, an earth mother, a domestic
    servant, and also dumber than he is),
Then I want to become a
Women's Liberation Movement woman.

And after I contemplate
No marriage, no family, no shaving under my arms,
And no one to step on a cockroach whenever I need him,
Then I don't.

THE
GOURMET

My husband grew up eating lox in New Jersey,
But now he eats saumon fumé.
The noshes he once used to nosh before dinner
He's calling hors d'oeuvres variés.
And food is cuisine since he learned how to be a gourmet.

He now has a palate instead of a stomach
And must have his salad après,
His ris de veau firm, and his port salut runny,
All ordered, of course, en français,
So the waiter should know he is serving a full-fledged gourmet.

No meal is complete without something en croute, a-
Mandine, béchamel, en gelée,
And those wines he selects with the care that a surgeon
Transplanting a heart might display.
He keeps sniffing the corks since he learned how to be a gourmet.

The tans some folks get from a trip to St. Thomas
He gets from the cerises flambés,
After which he requires, instead of a seltzer,
A cognac or Grand Marnier,
With a toast to the chef from my husband the nouveau gourmet.

The words people use for a Chartres or a Mozart
He's using to praise a soufflé.
He reads me aloud from James Beard and Craig Claiborne
The way others read from Corneille.
And he's moved by a mousse since he learned how to be a gourmet.

But back in New Jersey, whenever we visit,
They don't know from pouilly-fuissé.
They're still serving milk in the glass from the jelly.
They still cook the brisket all day.
And a son who can't finish three helpings is not a gourmet.

LESSONS

She was taught
If you don't get married you'll wind up a very lonely person staring at
    the four walls, and
He was taught
If you don't finish law school you'll wind up an object of pity and contempt
    selling ties in an East Orange haberdashery, and
She was taught
If you don't put a little something aside every week you'll wind up a
    very lonely person being thrown out on the sidewalk, and
He was taught
If you lend a friend your sport jacket he'll perspire under the arms and
    it won't come out at the cleaners and you'll wind up resentful, and
She was taught
If you don't have Blue Cross and Blue Shield you'll wind up a very lonely
    person delirious in a hospital ward, and
He was taught
If you go to bed with girls they'll lie and say they're pregnant and you'll
    wind up having to marry them, but
She changed her name to Maya, and
He changed his name to Orféo, and
They're living in a commune in the country
With collective housekeeping and organically grown vegetables and the kinds
    of shatteringly honest relationships
That are only possible between men and women
Who have renounced flush toilets and the telephone company, and
As a result of working in the fields, and
Washing in the streams, and
Wearing simple homespun robes they
Have freed their senses from the tyranny of the intellect, and
Tuned in to the music of the cosmos, and
Plumbed the secret depths of their innermost beings, but
She's still putting a little something aside every week, and
He's still not lending his jacket...
Just in case.

A BEAUTIFUL PERSON

Her exercise classes are putting new tone in her muscles.
Her skin doctor's scraping off all the old skin from her face.
Her colorist just changed her hair from champagne to peach melba.
And as soon as her glands are replaced at the clinic in Zurich,
Audrey my girlfriend is going to be
A Beautiful Person.

She's buying the co-op that Charlotte Ford once almost lived in.
She's buying the dresses that Women's Wear says Jackie wears.
She's buying a dog who's a niece of the Duchess of Windsor's,
And as soon as she's had an affair with Mike Nichols' third cousin,
Audrey my girlfriend is going to be
A Beautiful Person.

A very now rock group is playing at all of her parties.
A very now underground filmmaker's filming her thumbs.
A very now artist is doing her portrait in latex.
And as soon as Cesar Chavez comes to stay for the week end,
Audrey my girlfriend is going to be
A Beautiful Person.

She's learning the right things to want at the Parke-Bernet gallery.
She's learning the right way to eat and pronounce a coquille.
She's learning what charity balls have the chicest diseases.
And as soon as she's found someone chic-er than me to make friends with,
Audrey my girlfriend is going to be
A Beautiful Person.

REMEMBRANCE OF CHRISTMAS PAST

They let the children out of school too early.
I left the Christmas shopping till too late.
Each day we had a holiday excursion,
Which gave us the entire week to wait in line for
Movies by Disney,
Gift-wrapping by Lord & Taylor,
And everyone's restrooms.

On Christmas Eve we started to assemble
The easy-to-assemble telescope
And fire truck with forty-seven pieces.
By midnight it was plain there was no hope without
An astronomer,
A mechanical engineer,
And two psychiatrists.

We rose at dawn to three boys singing Rudolph.
We listened numbly to their shouts of glee.
The kitten threw up tinsel on the carpet.
The fire truck collided with the tree, requiring
One rug shampoo,
Several Band-aids,
And Scotch before breakfast.

I bought my husband shirts—wrong size, wrong colors,
And ties he said he couldn't be caught dead in.
I'd hinted Saint Laurent or something furry.
He bought me flannel gowns to go to bed in, also
A Teflon frying pan,
A plaid valise,
And The Weight Watchers Cook Book.

The turkey was still frozen at eleven.
At noon my eldest boy spilled Elmer's glue.
At five I had a swell Excedrin headache,
The kind that lasts till January two...but
Merry Christmas
And Happy New Year,
I think.

IDA, THE ONE WHO SUFFERS

Whatever happens to me
Has already happened to Ida, the one who suffers,
Only worse,
And with complications,
And her surgeon said it's a miracle she survived,
And her team of lawyers is suing for half a million,
And her druggist gave a gasp when he read the prescription,
And her husband swore he never saw such courage,
Because (though it may sound like bragging) she's not a complainer,
Which is why the nurse was delighted to carry her bedpan,
And her daughter flew home from the sit-in in order to visit,
And absolute strangers were begging to give blood donations,
And the man from Prudential even had tears in his eyes,
Because (though it may sound like bragging) everyone loves her,
Which is why both her sisters were phoning on day rates from Dayton,
And her specialist practically forced her to let him make house calls,
And the lady who cleans kept insisting on coming in Sundays,
And the cousins have canceled the Cousins Club annual meeting,
And she's almost embarrassed to mention how many presents
Keep arriving from girlfriends who love her all over the country,
All of them eating their hearts out with worry for Ida,
The one who suffers
The way other people
Enjoy.

SANDRA SHAPIRO IS SUCH A GOOD MOTHER

Sandra Shapiro is such a good mother. She says
That if she exposes her children to Winnie the Pooh and
    The Nutcracker Suite and the Hayden Planetarium,
They'll be accepted at Harvard. And she says
That if she exposes her children to black people and poor
    people and Jewish people who are married to non-Jewish
    people,
They'll vote Democratic. And she says
That if she teaches her children (frankly and openly and
    affirmationally) that having babies is a wonderful
    experience but not yet,
They'll thank her someday for being
Such a good mother.

Sandra Shapiro is such a good mother. She says
That if she takes her children on nice wholesome family
    outings like picnics and bike rides,
They won't smoke pot. And she says
That if she buys her children jigsaw puzzles and coloring
    books instead of machine guns and cowboy guns and death-
    ray guns,
They won't invade Indochina. And she says
That if she teaches her children (firmly and fearlessly and
    uncompromisingly) to always follow the dictates of their
    conscience but not yet,
They'll thank her someday for being
Such a good mother.

Sandra Shapiro is such a good mother. She says
That if she assures her children that they don't have to spend
    a single penny of their allowance on her birthday present
    unless they truly want to,
They'll truly want to. And she says
That if she assures her children that while she would never
    dream of prying she is warmly interested in anything they
    might want to tell her,
They'll tell her everything. And she says
That if she teaches her children (humbly and modestly and self-
    effacingly) that they'll thank her someday for being
Such a good mother,
Maybe someday they'll thank her,
But not yet.

SWAPPING

I like to keep up with the new aberrations
And here's what I recently read:
The latest in lust is the swapping of spouses.
The old-fashioned marriage, it's said,
Is just for the frigid, repressed, and neurotic,
Which no modern wife wants to be.
But nobody asks can he swap with my husband.

Is something the matter with me?

It's claimed that the switching of partners produces
A soundness of body and mind
And feelings of intimate group satisfaction
That couples can't manage to find
In cook-outs and bridge clubs and zoning board meetings
And fund drives to build the school gym.
But nobody asks will I swap her my husband.

Is something the matter with him?

Abandoned, insatiable, pulsing with hunger,
It all seems a terrible strain.
Now why did they have to go make things so fancy
When I've been enjoying them plain?
Erotica hasn't appeared at our parties.
We're still talking kids and clogged pipes.
And nobody asks can we swap with each other.

I guess we don't look like the types.

29

Murray the man of fashion
Is a former nebish from Nutley
Who has started having eager editorial assistants with their own
    apartments and narrow hips
Instead of having reluctant dental assistants with three roommates and
    heavy thighs
Since he found that he could convey,
By the length of his hair and the pattern and width of his ties,
Intellectual commitment, and
Sexual appetite, and
An offbeat but incredibly discerning lifestyle.

Murray the man of fashion
Has given up loafers with tassels
And is now spending the Fourth of July in the right part of East
    Hampton with producers of television specials
Instead of spending Memorial Day in the wrong part of Atlantic City
    with uncles and aunts
Since he found that he could convey,
By the nip in the waist of his jacket, the flare of his pants,
Psychological audacity, and
Moral superiority, and
A devastating but incredibly subtle wit.

Murray the man of fashion
Is no longer seen in white sweat socks
And is currently being invited to movie previews and art openings
    which are often reported in the metropolitan press
Instead of being invited to bar mitzvahs and unveilings which are often
    reported in letters from his mother to her sister Gert
Since he found that he could convey,
By the shade and the spacing and size of the stripes in his shirt,
That maybe he never heard
Of places like Nutley.

LOVE STORY

When Jenny my sitter got married to Herb
They agreed she would keep her own name.
Fidelity wasn't important, they said.
And he'd do the dusting while she earned the bread.
And they certainly wouldn't have babies. Instead,
They'd adopt.

She promised to master the tire and jack.
He promised to weep without shame.
(For males must express their emotions, they said.)
And she'd get a Master's while he baked the bread.
And they wouldn't be shocked to find three in their bed.
They'd adapt.

He married in bells, army surplus, and beard.
She married sans bra and sans shoes.
They gave all their presents to poor folks in Ghent.
And she swore if next season their union was rent
That she'd starve before even so much as a cent
She'd accept.

They left on their Yamaha happily stoned.
We're waiting to hear the bad news.
Assured, of course, it will never work out
Since they haven't a clue what real life is about
And besides, if they make it, we'll all start to doubt
Everything.

DECAY

There are laugh lines on my face but I'm not laughing.
I start yawning if I'm out much after twelve.
The latest dances give me lower back pain
And what's sitting on the shelves of my medicine chest I won't
    even discuss.

Excessive garlic irritates my colon.
Excessive coffee irritates my nerves.
Eight specialists are working on my problems
And it suddenly occurs to me that they now call my beauty marks
    moles.

The parts of me that proudly pointed upward
Are slowly taking on a downward droop.
I'm puffing when I reach the second landing
And I know Group Health rates better than I know everything I
    wanted to know about sex.

My shoulder's getting stiffer with each season.
The small print's getting blurrier each week.
The systems which I counted on forever
Are surrendering to creaks, leaks, blockages, and never mind
    what else.

The woman in my head is young and perfect.
The real one has to buy supportive hose.
So I'm waiting for serenity and wisdom,
Which, I'm assured, are supposed to make me feel much better
    about this whole thing.

THE FIRST FULL-FLEDGED FAMILY REUNION

The first full-fledged family reunion
Was held at the seashore
With 9 pounds of sturgeon
7 pounds of corned beef
1 nephew who got the highest mark on an intelligence test ever
    recorded in Hillside, New Jersey
4 aunts in pain taking pills
1 cousin in analysis taking notes
1 sister-in-law who makes a cherry cheese cake a person would
    be happy to pay to eat
5 uncles to whom what happened in the stock market shouldn't
    happen to their worst enemy
1 niece who is running away from home the minute the orthodontist
    removes her braces
1 cousin you wouldn't believe it to look at him only likes fellows
1 nephew involved with a person of a different racial persuasion
    which his parents are taking very well
1 brother-in-law with a house so big you could get lost and
    carpeting so thick you could suffocate and a mortgage so high
    you could go bankrupt
1 uncle whose wife is a saint to put up with him
1 cousin who has made such a name for himself he was almost
    Barbra Streisand's obstetrician
1 cousin who has made such a name for himself he was almost
    Jacob Javits' CPA
1 cousin don't ask what he does for a living
1 niece it wouldn't surprise anyone if next year she's playing
    at Carnegie Hall
1 nephew it wouldn't surprise anyone if next year he's
    sentenced to Leavenworth
2 aunts who go to the same butcher as Philip Roth's mother
And me wanting approval from all of them.

A LOT TO GIVE EACH OTHER

He was born before television, and
She was born after running boards, and
He was born before Saran Wrap, and
She was born after the cha cha, and
Although he isn't quite sure which one is Ringo and which one
    is Paul, and
She isn't quite sure which ones are the Andrews Sisters and which
    ones are the Mills Brothers,
They feel they've got a lot to give each other.

He worries about his prostate, and
She worries about her acne, and
He worries about good investments, and
She worries about bad vibrations, and
Although he isn't quite sure which one is Tom Hayden and which
    one is Peter Fonda, and
She isn't quite sure which one is Adolf Hitler and which one
    is Don Ameche,
They feel they've got a lot to give each other.

He doesn't relate to astrology, and
She doesn't relate to deodorants, and
He doesn't relate to acid, and
She doesn't relate to Gelusil, and
Although he isn't quite sure which one is Woodstock and which
    one is Hesse, and
She isn't quite sure which one is Pearl Harbor and which one
    is Veronica Lake,
They feel they've got a lot to give each other.

She wants the baby after they're married, and
He wants the baby before they're married, and
She wants a high-rise with an answering service and doormen, and
He wants a crash pad with mattresses and Weathermen, and
Although they aren't quite sure which one adjusted and which
    one sold out,
They feel they've got a lot to give each other.

ANTI-
HEROINE

I'd planned to be Heathcliff's Cathy, Lady Brett,
Nicole or Dominique or Scarlett O'Hara.
I hadn't planned to be folding up the laundry
In uncombed hair and last night's smudged mascara,
An expert on buying Fritos, cleaning the cat box,
Finding lost sneakers, playing hide-and-seek,
And other things unknown to Heathcliff's Cathy,
Scarlett, Lady Brett, and Dominique.

Why am I never running through the heather?
Why am I never raped by Howard Roark?
Why am I never going to Pamplona
Instead of Philadelphia and Newark?
How did I ever wind up with an Irving
When what I'd always had in mind was Rhett,
Or someone more appropriate to Cathy,
Dominique, Nicole, or Lady Brett.

I saw myself as heedless, heartless, headstrong,
An untamed woman searching for her mate.
And there he is—with charcoal, fork, and apron,
Prepared to broil some hot dogs on the grate.
I haven't wrecked his life or his digestion
With unrequited love or jealous wrath. He
Doesn't know that secretly I'm Scarlett,
Dominique, Nicole, or Brett, or Cathy.

Why am I never cracking up in Zurich?
Why am I never languishing on moors?
Why am I never spoiled by faithful mammys
Instead of spraying ant spray on the floors?
The tricycles are cluttering my foyer.
The Pop Tart crumbs are sprinkled on my soul.
And every year it's harder to be Cathy,
Dominique, Brett, Scarlett, and Nicole.

THE WORLD TRAVELER

I wish I were one of those spunky women
Who dash off to Africa
With a cleverly packed overnight bag and a pith helmet
Without always thinking
Is there a dentist,
And can I buy Kleenex,
And where will I find the name
Of a good dry cleaners.

I wish I were one of those spunky women
Who climb the Matterhorn,
And race Maseratis,
And run barefoot through the Bois de Boulogne,
Without always thinking
That I'll step on a rusty nail
And need a tetanus shot.

I wish I were one of those spunky women
Who travel around the world on freighters,
And fight in doomed revolutions,
And sleep with some dark stranger in Algiers,
Without always thinking
That the stranger will talk about me
In New Jersey.

I wish I were one of those spunky women...
But as I sit here on this plane from Dulles to London,
With twenty pounds of overweight in aspirin,
A heating pad and Tums and Kaopectate,
And throat spray and an extra pair of glasses
(Suppose the first pair breaks in a pub in Chelsea?),
Wondering whether the sitter's rejecting my children
And whether I'll go down in flames reading Time magazine,
Then it all seems a high price to pay
Just to be
Spunky.

DOWN AND
OUT IN
LONDON

In London I didn't see the Beatles.
In London I didn't see the Stones.
In London I didn't see Peter Sellers telling mod kinky stories
    to Princess Margaret and Anthony Armstrong-Jones
While internationally famous hairdressers
And internationally skinny models
Did corrupt but trendy things to each other
At private clubs.

In London I saw Museums and Towers.
In London I saw them change the guard.
In London I ate a lot of meat pies with one piece of meat
    blended with three pounds of lard,
Followed by a walk in the rain
And another one of those afternoon teas
With the shredded lettuce leaves
On tissue paper.

In London I'd planned to change my image.
In London I haven't changed a thing.
In London I'm standing on the King's Road
With wet feet,
Indigestion,
The wrong hemline,
A run in my pantyhose,
The Oxford Book of English Verse,
And a continuing inability to swing
Even in London.

OUT ON
THE ALPS

As daylight breaks over the Alps (Courchevel 1850),
And the right thing to do is roll over and sleep until ten,
My husband is nudging my black-and-blue thigh with his kneecap,
And saying (hey, great!) that it's time to go skiing again.
So I put on the stretch pants that quit stretching over my
    stomach
When I learned how to eat seven courses at lunch and diner,
Then I put on the sweaters, the parka, the hood, and the ski
    boots
(They're hell in the morning but tend to get worse through the
    day),
And I leave the warm room with its blankets and Agatha Christies
To go where it's snowy and windy and cold and not safe,
Ignoring the pain in my shoulders, arms, thighs, calves, and
    ankles,
Plus the place where the heel in my boot is beginning to chafe.
And we're off in the télécabine to the top of the mountain
And I'm hoping the motor won't stop as we sway over peaks,
And the cable won't snap as we hang forty feet from abysses,
And that terrible sound is the wind and not somebody's shrieks.
Now (isn't it lovely!) we're here with the treetops below us.
And my skis aren't on but already I've fallen down twice
Just from taking a look at the trail—narrow, vertical, fatal.
(And here comes my husband, Jean-Claude, with some words of
    advice.)
Well, I've just cut my thumb in the process of closing my
    bindings,
And my goggles are fogged and my nerves inexpressibly shot.
But I'm off with a wild snowplow turn and a large crowd of
    Frenchmen
Who keep schussing past me with shouts of à gauche and à droite.
And I know I could tell which was which if I wasn't attempting
To bend at the knees, shift my weight, not go over that ledge,
Which explains why I've skied off the trail and am presently
    standing
In uncharted mountains and up to my fesses in the neige,
Where I'm dreaming of tropical isles, riding surf in bikinis,
But willing to settle for home, pushing kids in the carriage,
And firmly convinced that the Alps may be swell for the Killys,
But not for a person who's only a skier by marriage.

David is dying to get married.
He is dying to share
His heart, his insights, and the unspoiled island in the
    Caribbean where he is the only American who goes there
With someone feminine enough and intelligent enough and mature enough
    to understand
That when he's hostile it's because he's feeling threatened,
And when he's vicious it's because he feels unloved,
And when he's paranoid, sadistic, depressed, or sexually inadequate,
It's simply because
She has failed him. Yes,
David is dying to get married.
He is dying to share
His fishtank, his discounts, and the unspoiled restaurant in
    Chinatown where he is the only Caucasian who eats there
With someone secure enough and subtle enough and grateful enough
    to understand
That when he's rigid it's because he has high standards,
And when he's violent it's because he has no choice,
And when he's manic, suicidal, or having trouble sleeping,
It's simply because
She has failed him. Yes,
David is dying to get married.
To a woman like Lauren Bacall but a bit more submissive.
To a woman like Melina Mercouri but a bit more refined.
To a woman who understands that in order to share
His loves, his hates, his hopes, his fears, his low license plate,
    his high tax bracket, and his rent-controlled apartment with
    the terrace where he and his mother are the only people who
    live there,
She'd better not fail him.

Starting on Monday I'm living on carrots and bouillon.
Starting on Monday I'm bidding the bagel adieu.
I'm switching from Hersheys with almonds to gaunt and anemic,
And people will ask me could that skinny person be you.
I'll count every calorie from squash (half a cup, 47)
To Life Saver (8), stalk of celery (5), pepper ring (2),
Starting on Monday.

Starting on Monday I'll jog for a mile in the morning.
(That's after the sit-ups and push-ups and touching my toes.)
The gratification I once used to seek in lasagna
I'll find on the day that I have to go buy smaller clothes.
I'll turn my attention from infantile pleasures like Clark Bars
To things like the song of a bird and the scent of a rose,
Starting on Monday.

Starting on Monday my will will be stronger than brownies,
And anything more than an unsalted egg will seem crude.
My inner-thigh fat and my upper-arm flab will diminish.
My cheeks will be hollowed, my ribs will begin to protrude.
The bones of my pelvis will make their initial appearance —
A testament to my relentless abstention from food,
Starting on Monday.

But Tuesday a friend came for coffee and brought homemade muffins.
And Wednesday I had to quit jogging because of my back.
On Thursday I read in the paper an excess of egg yolk
Would clog up my vessels and certainly cause an attack.
On Friday we ate at the Goldfarbs. She always makes cream sauce,
And always gets sulky if people don't eat what she makes.
On Saturday evening we went with the kids to a drive-in.
I begged for a Fresca but all they were selling were shakes.
On Sunday my stomach oozed over the top of my waistband,
And filled with self-loathing I sought consolation in pie
And the thought that Onassis could bribe me with yachts and with emeralds
But still I'd refuse to taste even a single French fry . . .
Starting on Monday.

ALAN
THE
DROP-
OUT

My cousin Alan the drop-out
Is giving the family such heartache
That already he's caused one angina,
A skin rash, and plenty of migraines,
And it's clear that he's killing his mother,
According to mine.

My cousin Alan the drop-out,
With brains like an Einstein or Goldberg
And a guaranteed future in Orlon,
Is living in worse than a cellar
With a girlfriend a mother could die from,
According to mine.

My cousin Alan the drop-out,
Who dressed like a playboy from Florida
And everyone swore was Rock Hudson,
Now looks like King Kong with a headband,
And a mother could faint just to see him,
According to mine.

My cousin Alan the drop-out,
A person who once wouldn't jaywalk,
Keeps going to jail like a Scarface
For doing fresh things to the System,
And the shame gives his mother hot flashes,
According to mine.

My cousin Alan the drop-out,
Is writing his memoirs for Harper's
And people in suits want his viewpoint
On stations both local and network.
He's posing for pictures at Newsweek
And auditions tomorrow for Susskind,
And his mother could learn to enjoy it,
According to mine.

THE LADY
NEXT DOOR

The lady next door,
Who weighs eight pounds less than I do
And wears peach face gleamer and tawny lip gloss to take out
the garbage,
Has lately been looking at my husband
As if he were someone like Robert Redford,
And she were someone like Ali MacGraw,
And I were someone like Mother of the Year.

The lady next door,
Whose children go to analysts and Choate,
And whose favorite drink is a dry white burgundy with a smidgen
of crème de cassis,
Has lately been looking at my husband
As if he were someone with inexpressible yearnings,
And she were someone who majored in how to express them,
And I were someone who played a lot of hockey.

The lady next door,
Has lately been looking at my husband,
Who has lately been looking back,
Leaving me to contemplate
Murder,
Suicide,
Adult education courses,
An affair with one of those rich Greek eighty-year-olds who
prefer younger women,
An affair with one of those alienated twenty-year-olds who prefer
older women,
Or maybe an affair
With the man next door,
Who has Cardin suits, a rapier wit, a Ferrari,
As well as close friends in the arts,
And who has lately been looking at me
As if I were someone who knew how to sew on buttons,
And he were someone who needed someone to sew them,
And my husband were only someone who deserved
The lady next door.

POLITICALLY PERFECT

Sally and Stu
Were married by a militant minister
(He was bitten by a Birmingham police dog),
Moved to an integrated neighborhood
(Thirty-four per cent were Black or Other),
Turned down a low-cost trip to Greece
(For obvious reasons),

And have always strived to be
Politically perfect
By displaying aggressive bumper stickers,
Boycotting non-returnable bottles,
And including, at every cocktail party,
One American Indian, one Draft Resister, and Ralph Nader.

Sally and Stu
Were admitted to the nicest New Left circles
(Published writers, sometimes even Mailer),
Solicited for all the finest causes
(Panthers, Moratoriums, Defense Funds),
Advocated the dismantling of the war machine and the smashing of the
    major corporations and the total restructuring of society
(Without, of course, condoning undue violence),
And have always strived to be
Politically perfect
By giving generously,
Picketing profusely,
And including, at every Christmas party,
One unwed mother, one well-intentioned bomber, and the maid.

They have always strived to be
Politically perfect—but

Recently they met a sweet policeman
And a rotten revolutionary,
And started feeling hostile to all muggers
Regardless of color or creed,
And then he discovered that he couldn't say "pig" or "right on"
Without sounding insincere,
And then she discovered that she couldn't say "male sexist oppressor"
Without sounding insincere,
And when he asked her
Was she capable of taking off her clothes and painting an anti-war symbol on
    her stomach and floating across the Potomac in the interests of world peace,
And her answer was no,
And when she asked him
Was he capable of annihilating his racist parents and his racist brother Arnold
    and that racist little blonde he used to go with in the interests of
    world brotherhood,
And his answer was no,
They knew
They'd never be
Politically perfect.

THE
WRITERS

I write in the bedroom with unsorted laundry,
A crib, and a baby who hollers.
My husband the writer gets gold velvet chairs,
A couch that cost four hundred dollars,
A wall-to-wall carpet, bright red and all wool,
And a desk big enough to play pool on.

I type in quadruplicate, two sets for me
And two for the baby to drool on,
In a setting conducive to grocery lists
And decisions like chopped steak or flounder.
Did Emily Dickinson have to write poems
With diaper-rash ointment around her?
Did Elizabeth Browning stop counting the ways
When Robert said one hot pastrami?
Excuse me, the big boys just came home from school
And they're yelling their heads off for mommy.

My husband the writer makes long-distance calls
To people too famous to mention.
The closest I get to the great outside world
Is listening on the extension
Or reading old Digests while taking the kids
For their flu shots and antibiotics.
(Everyone knows that the mother who works
Will doubtlessly bring up psychotics
Unless she's right there when the chicken pox pop
Or they're stricken with gnat bites and toe aches.)
Did Edna St. Vincent Millay rise at dawn
For a first-grade production called Snowflakes?
Did Marianne Moore put her symbols aside
To wipe Quaker Oats off the table?
Excuse me, my husband would like a cold beer.
I'll be back just as soon as I'm able.

The baby is sleeping, the beds have been made,
And I've mopped where the kitchen was muddy.
My husband the writer has finished the Times
And he's vanishing into his study,
Where no one would dare to disturb his deep thoughts
(Or the half-hour nap he requires).
I've gone to the cleaners and picked up dessert
And I even put air in the tires
Before sitting down at my second-hand Royal.
(He just bought a new Olivetti.)
Did Miss Amy Lowell find Patterns besmirched
With dribbles of Junior Spaghetti?
Does Phyllis McGinley refrain from her rhymes
Whenever her garden needs spraying?
Excuse me, the dishwasher's gone on the blink.
Maybe I'll switch to crocheting.

WHEN I
GROW UP

When I grow up I'll stop believing.
That if Paul Newman really got to know me he'd divorce Joanne
    Woodward,
And I'll stop believing
That it wouldn't be so impossible for a teenage boy to mistake
    me for a teenage girl,
And I'll stop believing
That someday I'll find a beauty cream which, after I massage it
    gently into my skin every night for three weeks before retiring,
You'll never recognize me.
When I grow up I'll stop believing
That people who own paintings of blobs and stripes have a better
    grasp of the universe than people who own paintings of sunsets,
And I'll stop believing
That people who buy VWs and Volvos are intrinsically more humane
    than people who buy Lincoln Continentals,
And I'll stop believing
That people who admire people like Dick Cavett have nobler
    aspirations
Than people who admire Johnny Carson.
When I grow up I'll stop believing
That the Mafia is run by distinguished-looking gentlemen with graying
    temples and wonderful home lives,
And I'll stop believing
That the Republican party is run by insincere-looking gentlemen
    with short socks and terrible sex lives,
And I'll stop believing
That an Episcopalian is anyone who knew about sailboats, napkin
    rings, Hepplewhite, and self-assurance
Twenty years before I did.
When I grow up I'll stop believing
That I'm destined to become the toast of Broadway,
And I'll stop believing
That I'm destined to become the Dean of Smith,
And I'll stop believing
That I'm destined to become a love goddess, a tennis champion,
    Madame Curie, or Golda Meir
When I grow up.

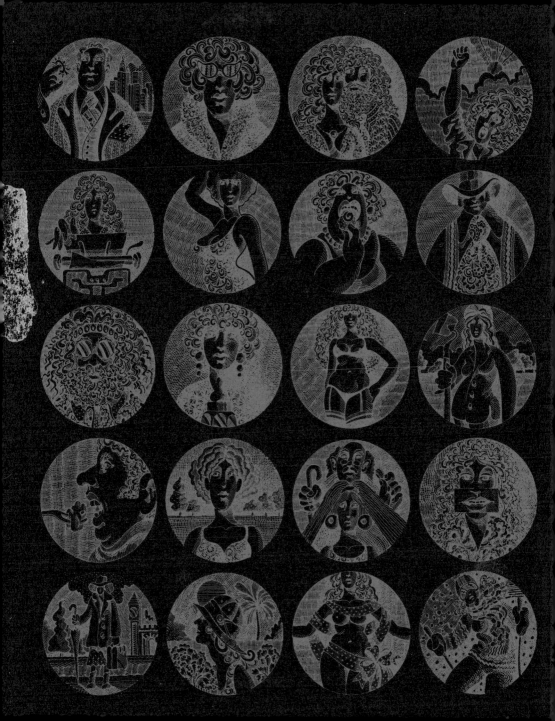